Hey Lord, This Isn't What I Ordered!

Hey Lord, This Isn't What I Ordered!

ISBN-13: 978-1-58173-576-5
ISBN-10: 1-58173-576-6

Book design by Pat Covert
Cover photo © Royalty-Free/Corbis

Printed in the United States of America

Hey Lord, This Isn't What I Ordered!

FaithPoint PRESS

There Are No Guarantees

My grandma once told me, "If you want a guarantee, buy a toaster." We were in a restaurant, I remember, and I was whining because there was too much mayonnaise on my sandwich. "Hey, Lord," I was thinking to myself grumpily, "this isn't what I ordered."

What my grandma said didn't immediately sink in. It only made me grumpier, in fact. I used to complain a lot about little things. Still do. But something changed when my grandma passed away. When some stupid little thing got me down, I heard her voice again, asking me what in the heck I HAD ordered from God. Had I ordered up a perfect life for myself? One in which nothing ever went awry? Did I expect everyone to act the way I planned? Did I think the world should operate according to my rules?

You see, I finally realized with considerable horror just how awful a world like that would be. I finally realized (duh) that I was not in charge. Most importantly, I didn't want to be!

I hope this little book will make you laugh as you work your way through that stuff you didn't order from God. It's full of quotes from famous and not-so-famous people, and even some totally anonymous ones. I've arranged them by subject so you can find the ones that apply to what's happening to you right now. And maybe you'll find just the right thought to make you laugh and move on. To cope a little bit better with the flat tires, the overcooked steak, the screaming kids, the bad hair days. Even the really sad stuff—the losses and the tragedies. Laughing about it helps me remember that I'm not in charge and that there are no guarantees. But somehow it all works out in the end. At least that's what Grandma says.

Ellen Patrick

Table of Contents

Aches & Pains

If you don't do what's best for your
body, you're the one who comes
up on the short end.
Julius Erving

Warning: Humor may be hazardous
to your illness.
Ellie Katz

Minor surgery is surgery
someone else is having.
Joseph Cook

Old people have fewer diseases than the
young, but their diseases never leave them.
Hippocrates

Drugs don't work in patients
who don't take them.
C. Everett Koop

I don't deserve this; but I have arthritis,
and I don't deserve that either.
Jack Benny

Bacteria keep us from heaven
and put us there.
Martin H. Fischer

It requires a great deal of faith for a man
to be cured by his own placebos.
John L. McClenahan

Cured yesterday of my disease, I died
last night of my physician.
Matthew Prior

If I'd known I was going to live this long,
I'd have taken better care of myself.
Eubie Blake

God heals and the doctor takes the fee.
Benjamin Franklin

My doctor recently told me that jogging could add years to my life. I think he was right. I feel ten years older already.
Milton Berle

My illness is due to my doctor's insistence that I drink milk, a whitish fluid they force down helpless babies.
W. C. Fields

Adversity

Adversity causes some men to break; others to break records.
William A. Ward

There's no easy way out. If there were, I would have bought it. And believe me, it would be one of my favorite things!
Oprah Winfrey

If joy were the only emotion God intended us to feel, He could just zap us and take us to heaven right now. The truth is that our trials are a furnace forging us into gold.
Barbara Johnson

In order to be walked on,
you have to be lying down.
Brian Weir

When I hear somebody say, "Life is hard," I am always tempted to ask, "Compared to what?"
Sydney J. Harris

—

Trouble knocked at the door, but, hearing laughter, hurried away.
Benjamin Franklin

—

A bend in the road is not the end of the road ... unless you fail to make the turn.

—

What a pity human beings can't exchange problems. Everyone knows exactly how to solve the other fellow's.
Olin Miller

If you break your neck, if you
have nothing to eat, if your house
is on fire, then you got a problem.
Everything else is inconvenience.
Robert Fulghum

Pain is inevitable. Suffering is optional.
M. Kathleen Casey

It just wouldn't be a picnic
without the ants.

When the world drops you to your knees,
take the opportunity to pray!

"Difficulty" is not a word to be found in the dictionary of heaven. Nothing can be impossible with God.
Charles H. Spurgeon

Challenges are gifts that force us to search for a new center of gravity. Don't fight them. Just find a different way to stand.
Oprah Winfrey

People think that Christians have no problems. No worries and no strife, but Christian life isn't easy—that's why it's still called life.
Kurios

Aging

If you live to be one hundred, you've got it made. Very few people die past that age.
George Burns

It is after you have lost your teeth that you can afford to buy steaks.
Pierre August Renoir

I don't know how you feel about old age ... but in my case I didn't even see it coming. It hit me from the rear.
Phyllis Diller

First you forget names, then you
forget faces, then you forget to pull
your zipper up, then you forget
to pull your zipper down.

Welcome [birthdays] as mile-markers that
remind you that you aren't home yet, but
you're closer than you've ever been.
Max Lucado

There has been an alarming increase in the
number of things I know nothing about!

Old age ain't no place for sissies.
Bette Davis

As a graduate of the Zsa Zsa Gabor
School of Creative Mathematics, I
honestly do not know how old I am.
Erma Bombeck

Thirty-five is when you finally get
your head together and your
body starts falling apart.
Caryn Leschen

I'm so old they've cancelled
my blood type.
Bob Hope

As you get older three things happen.
The first is your memory goes, and
I can't remember the other two.
Norman Wisdom

—

Thirty was so strange for me. I've really
had to come to terms with the fact that I
am now a walking and talking adult.
C. S. Lewis

—

A sweet old lady stays active all her life. A
grumpy old grouch sits and rocks.

—

As we grow older, our bodies get shorter
and our anecdotes longer.
Robert Quillen

He's so old that when he orders a
three-minute egg, they ask for
the money upfront.
Milton Berle

The four stages of man are infancy,
childhood, adolescence, and obsolescence.
Art Linkletter

To me, old age is fifteen years
older than I am.

My mother always used to say:
"The older you get, the better you get …
unless you're a banana."
Rose Nylund

The secret to staying young is to live
honestly, eat slowly, and lie about your age.
Lucille Ball

Old men are fond of giving good advice,
to console themselves for being no longer
in a position to give bad examples.
François La Rochefoucauld

Growing old is mandatory;
growing up is optional.
Chili Davis

Youth is when you're allowed to stay up late on New Year's Eve. Middle age is when you're forced to.
Bill Vaughn

There is only one cure for gray hair. It was invented by a Frenchman. It is called the guillotine.
P. G. Wodehouse

The elderly don't drive that badly; they're just the only ones with time to do the speed limit.
Jason Love

The long, dull, monotonous years of middle-aged prosperity or middle-aged adversity are excellent campaigning weather for the devil.
C. S. Lewis

Anger

If at the end of the day, you feel dog-tired, maybe it's because you growled all day.

If a small thing has the power to make you angry, does that not indicate something about your size?
Sydney J. Harris

Anger is only one letter short of danger.

A chip on the shoulder is a sure
sign of wood higher up.
Brigham Young

People who fly into a rage always
make a bad landing.
Will Rogers

Never go to bed mad. Stay up and fight.
Phyllis Diller

I don't know about you, but nothing makes me want to hurl a chair through the window and punch someone's lights out like being told I need anger management lessons.
Mark Steyn

Holding on to anger only gives you tense muscles.

Your anger is like the bubbles in a can of soda. The more you're shaken, the more you want to let it out. The longer you keep it in though, the greater the size of the eventual explosion—and the flatter the drink at the end.

Anger is never without reason,
but seldom a good one.
Benjamin Franklin

My recipe for dealing with anger and
frustration: set the kitchen timer for
twenty minutes, cry, rant, and rave, and at
the sound of the bell, simmer down and
go about business as usual.
Phyllis Diller

Anyone can become angry. That is easy.
But to be angry with the right person,
to the right degree, at the right time,
for the right purpose and in the
right way—that is not easy.
Aristotle

Anger is as a stone cast into a wasp's nest.

Men are like steel: when they lose their
temper, they lose their worth.
Chuck Norris

Irritability is immaturity of character. If
you are subject to being cross and
unpleasant with others for no apparent
reason, you need to come face-to-face
with the fact that you are thinking too
much of yourself. After all, your feelings
are not the most important thing
in this world.
Lawrence G. Lovasik

Apologizing

When you realize you've made a mistake, make amends immediately. It's easier to eat crow while it's still warm.
Dan Heist

Never ruin an apology with an excuse.
Kimberly Johnson

A stiff apology is a second insult. The injured party does not want to be compensated because he has been wronged; he wants to be healed because he has been hurt.
Gilbert K. Chesterton

Apology is a lovely perfume; it can transform the clumsiest moment into a gracious gift.
Margaret Lee Runbeck

The right sort of people do not want apologies, and the wrong sort take a mean advantage of them.
P. G. Wodehouse

An apology is the superglue of life. It can repair just about anything.
Lynn Johnston

Love in the real world means saying
you're sorry ten times a day.
Kathie Lee Gifford

An apology is a good way to
have the last word.

True remorse is never just a regret over
consequence; it is a regret over motive.
Mignon McLaughlin

Arguments

The Bible says that two cannot walk
together unless they are agreed.
Peter Akinola

Never argue with a fool—people might not know the difference.

Never argue at the dinner table, for the one who is not hungry always gets the best of the argument.
Richard Whately

Men should stop fighting among themselves and start fighting insects.
Luther Burbank

There are two theories to arguing with a woman. Neither one works.
Will Rogers

Arguments with furniture are
rarely productive.
Kehlog Albran

There are two sides to every argument,
unless a person is personally involved, in
which case there is only one.
Cutler Webster

I don't have to attend every
argument I'm invited to.

Whenever you accept my views,
I shall be in full agreement with you.

Those who agree with us may not be right, but we admire their astuteness.

———

In most instances, all an argument proves is that two people are present.

———

When arguing with a stone,
an egg is always wrong.
African Proverb

Attitude

Since the house is on fire,
let us warm ourselves.
Italian Proverb

Aim at heaven and you will get earth thrown in. Aim at earth and you get neither.
C. S. Lewis

—

A good thing to remember is somebody's got it a lot worse than we do.
Joel Osteen

—

If you want a guarantee, buy a toaster.

—

We cannot direct the wind, but we can adjust the sails.
Dolly Parton

A positive attitude may not solve all your problems, but it will annoy enough people to make it worth the effort.
Herm Albright

Every thought is a seed. If you plant crab apples, don't count on harvesting Golden Delicious.
Bill Meyer

Two men looked out from prison bars: one saw mud, the other saw stars.

The only disability in life is a bad attitude.
Scott Hamilton

When the only tool you own is a
hammer, every problem begins to
resemble a nail.
Abraham Maslow

Change

Pray and, while you pray, move your feet.
Quaker saying

If you don't like the road you're walking,
start paving another one.
Dolly Parton

Change is inevitable—
except from vending machines.
Robert C. Gallagher

Change is bouncing a ball on the
circumference of a circle.

The most damaging phrase in the
English language is: "It's always
been done that way."
Grace Hopper

People are very open-minded about
new things—as long as they're
exactly like the old ones.
Charles Kettering

You don't have to be the Dalai Lama to tell
people that life's about change.
John Cleese

It is not necessary to change.
Survival is not mandatory.
W. Edwards Deming

It is not necessary to change.

When you're finished changing,
you're finished.
Benjamin Franklin

Progress is a continuing effort to make
the things we eat, drink, and wear
as good as they used to be.
Bill Vaughn

No one likes change but babies in diapers.
Barbara Johnson

He who rejects change is the architect of decay. The only human institution which rejects progress is the cemetery.
Harold Wilson

If you always do what you've always done, you'll always be what you've always been.
Josh McDowell

There is nothing permanent except change.
Heraclitus

If you have always done it that way, it is probably wrong.
Charles Kettering

It's not so much that we're afraid of change or so in love with the old ways, but it's that place in between that we fear. … It's like being between trapezes. It's Linus when his blanket is in the dryer. There's nothing to hold on to.
Marilyn Ferguson

You will suddenly realize that the reason you never changed before was because you didn't want to.
Robert Schuller

God loves us just the way we are, but He loves us too much to leave us that way.
Max Lucado

Children

Have you any idea how many kids it takes to turn off one light in the kitchen? Three. It takes one to say, "What light?" and two more to say, "I didn't turn it on."
Erma Bombeck

Always end the name of your child with a vowel, so that when you yell, the name will carry.
Bill Cosby

Child rearing myth #1: Labor ends when the baby is born.

The main purpose of holding children's parties is to remind yourself that there are children more awful than your own.

If you desire to drain to the dregs the fullest cup of scorn and hatred that a fellow human being can pour out for you, let a young mother hear you call dear baby "it."
T. S. Eliot

Children: You spend the first two years of their life teaching them to walk and talk. Then you spend the next sixteen years telling them to sit down and shut up.
Phyllis Diller

43

The beauty of "spacing" children many years apart lies in the fact that parents have time to learn the mistakes that were made with the older ones—which permits them to make exactly the opposite mistakes with the younger ones.
Sydney J. Harris

Children are natural mimics who act like their parents despite every effort to teach them good manners.

A three-year-old child is a being who gets almost as much fun out of a fifty-six dollar set of swings as it does out of finding a small green worm.
Bill Vaughn

Children today are tyrants. They contradict their parents, gobble their food, and tyrannize their teachers.
Socrates

Never have more children than you have car windows.
Erma Bombeck

If you have a lot of tension, and you get a headache, do what it says on the aspirin bottle: "Take two aspirin" and "Keep away from children."

Having children is like having a bowling alley installed in your brain.
Martin Mull

Criticism

To make a criticism is a bit like complaining about the shape of the Pyramids.
Piers Brendon

He who flings mud loses a lot of ground.

When a man points a finger at someone else, he should remember that four of his fingers are pointing at himself.
Louis Nizer

Do what you feel in your heart to be right,
for you'll be criticized anyway.
Eleanor Roosevelt

The only gracious way to accept an insult
is to ignore it; if you can't ignore it, top it;
if you can't top it, laugh at it; if you can't
laugh at it, it's probably deserved.
Russell Lynes

Laugh at yourself first,
before anyone else can.
Elsa Maxwell

Do you have relatives that do nothing but complain and criticize? Don't let them get to you. God gave you two ears so things could go in one ear and out the other. Use them.
Kathy Laurenhue

Death

The difficulty about all this dying is that you can't tell a fellow anything about it, so where does the fun come in?
Alice James

Never knock on Death's door; ring the bell and run away! Death really hates that!
Matt Frewer

If even dying is to be made a social
function, then grant me the favor
of sneaking out on tiptoe without
disturbing the party.
Dag Hammarskjold

Death—To stop sinning suddenly.
Elbert Hubbard

I'm not afraid of death. It's the stake one
puts up in order to play the game of life.
Jean Giraudoux

---

100 percent of us die, and the percentage
cannot be increased.
C. S. Lewis

The idea is to die young as
late as possible.
Ashley Montagu

Death smiles at us all. All a man
can do is smile back.
Marcus Aurelius

The really frightening thing about
middle age is the knowledge that
you'll grow out of it.
Doris Day

If your time ain't come, not even
a doctor can kill you.
American Proverb

We all have to die some day,
if we live long enough.
Dave Farber

You can't get out of life alive.
Les Brown

Die? I should say not, dear fellow. No
Barrymore would allow such a
conventional thing to happen to him.
John Barrymore

Death is just nature's way of
telling you to slow down.
Dick Sharples

They say such nice things about people at their funerals that it makes me sad that I'm going to miss mine by just a few days.
Garrison Keillor

Death? Why this fuss about death? Use your imagination, try to visualize a world without death! Death is the essential condition of life, not an evil.
Charlotte Perkins Gilman

I had seen birth and death but had thought they were different.
T. S. Eliot

Dying is a very dull, dreary affair.
And my advice to you is to have
nothing whatever to do with it.
W. Somerset Maugham

At my age I do what Mark Twain did. I get
my daily paper, look at the obituaries page,
and if I'm not there, I carry on as usual.
Patrick Moore

For days after death, hair and fingernails
continue to grow, but phone
calls taper off.
Johnny Carson

We cannot truly face life until we face the
fact that it will be taken away from us.
Billy Graham

—

Why is it that we rejoice at birth and
grieve at a funeral? It is because
we are not the person involved.
Mark Twain

—

I am ready to meet my maker, but whether
my maker is prepared for the great ordeal
of meeting me is another matter.
Winston Churchill

Life is pleasant. Death is peaceful. It's the transition that's troublesome.
Isaac Asimov

I hate funerals and would not attend my own if it could be avoided.
Robert T. Morris

Afraid of death? Not at all. Be a great relief. Then I wouldn't have to talk to you.
Katharine Hepburn

Death is life's way of telling you you're fired.

Debt

The only man who sticks closer to you in adversity than a friend is a creditor.

———

Running into debt isn't so bad. It's running into creditors that hurts.

———

Bankruptcy is a legal proceeding in which you put your money in your pants pocket and give your coat to your creditors.
Joey Adams

———

If one wants to get out and stay out of debt, he should act his wage.

If you owe the bank $100, that's your problem. If you owe the bank $100 million, that's the bank's problem.
Jean Paul Getty

Bankruptcy stared me in the face, but one thought kept me calm: soon I'd be too poor to need an anti-theft alarm.
Gina Rothfels

Some debts are fun when you are acquiring them, but none are fun when you set about retiring them.
Ogden Nash

Depression

I had the blues
because I had no shoes,
until upon the street,
I met a man who had no feet.
Persian Proverb

If you were happy every day of your life,
you wouldn't be a human being; you'd be
a game show host.
Gabriel Heatter

Noble deeds and hot baths are the
best cures for depression.
Dodie Smith

Depression can be the sand that
makes the pearl.
Joni Mitchell

If you know someone who tries to drown
their sorrows, you might tell them
sorrows know how to swim.

This is my depressed stance. When you're
depressed, it makes a lot of difference how
you stand. The worst thing you can do is
straighten up and hold your head high
because then you'll start to feel better. If
you're going to get any joy out of being
depressed, you've got to stand like this.
Charles Schulz

Dieting

Life expectancy would grow by leaps
and bounds if green vegetables
smelled as good as bacon.
Doug Larson

Ｄ

What you eat standing up doesn't count.
Beth Barnes

Ｄ

"Thank you for calling the weight loss
hotline. If you would like to lose half a
pound right now, press 1 eighteen
thousand times."
Randy Glasbergen

I drive way too fast to worry
about cholesterol.

Older people shouldn't eat health
food. They need all the
preservatives they can get.
Robert Orben

Be careful about reading health books.
You may die of a misprint.
Mark Twain

Health nuts are going to feel stupid
someday, lying in hospitals
dying of nothing.
Redd Foxx

The cardiologist's diet: If it tastes good, spit it out.

———

Avoid fruits and nuts: after all, you are what you eat.
Garfield

———

The older you get, the harder it is to lose weight, because by then your body and your fat have become good friends.

———

My doctor told me to stop having intimate dinners for four. Unless there are three other people.
Orson Welles

A diet is the penalty we pay for exceeding the feed limit.

Don't dig your grave with your own knife and fork.
English Proverb

A moment on the lips can be a lifetime on the hips.
Sal Simeon

Never eat more than you can lift.
Miss Piggy

Eating rice cakes is like chewing on a foam coffee cup, only less filling.
Dave Barry

Food is essential to life; therefore, make it good.
S. Truett Cathy

When I buy cookies, I just eat four and throw the rest away. But first I spray them with Raid so I won't dig them out of the garbage later. Be careful, though, because that Raid really doesn't taste that bad.
Janette Barber

You can't lose weight by talking about it.
You have to keep your mouth shut!

Dieting is not a piece of cake.
Vegetables are a must on a diet. I
suggest carrot cake, zucchini
bread, and pumpkin pie.
Garfield

Divorce

When two people decide to get a divorce,
it isn't a sign that they "don't understand"
one another, but a sign that they
have, at last, begun to.
Helen Rowland

When a woman steals your husband,
there is no better revenge than
to let her keep him.

Love, the quest; marriage, the conquest;
divorce, the inquest.

Divorce is the psychological equivalent
of a triple coronary by-pass. After such
a monumental assault on the heart,
it takes years to amend all the habits
and attitudes that led up to it.
Mary Kay Blakely

The difference between a divorce and a legal separation is that a legal separation gives a husband time to hide his money.
Johnny Carson

In Hollywood, an equitable divorce settlement means each party getting 50 percent of publicity.
Lauren Bacall

She cried—and the judge wiped her tears with my checkbook.
Tommy Manville

When a couple decides to divorce, they should inform both sets of parents before having a party and telling their friends. This is not only courteous but practical. Parents may be very willing to pitch in with comments, criticism, and malicious gossip of their own to help the divorce along.
P. J. O'Rourke

Love is grand; divorce is a hundred grand.

Being divorced is like being hit by a Mack truck. If you live through it, you start looking very carefully to the right and to the left.
Jean Kerr

Doubt

There are two ways to slide easily
through life: to believe everything or to
doubt everything. Both ways save
us from thinking.
Alfred Korzybski

Doubt is the father of invention.
Galileo

If I discover within myself a desire which
no experience in this world can satisfy, the
most probable explanation is that I was
made for another world.
C. S. Lewis

Doubt is the vestibule through which
all must pass before they can enter
into the temple of wisdom.
Charles Caleb Colton

—

When in doubt, mumble; when in trouble,
delegate; when in charge, ponder.
James H. Boren

—

Don't put a question mark
where God put a period.

Egotism

Egotism is the anesthetic that
dulls the pain of stupidity.
Frank Leahy

Remember when a peacock struts
his stuff, he shows his backside
to half the world.
Herve Wiener

Egotism is the glue with which
you get stuck in yourself.
Dan Post

Egotism is an alphabet of one letter.

Excuses

We are all manufacturers. Making good,
making trouble, or making excuses.
H. V. Adolt

We are all manufacturers. Making good, making trouble, or making excuses.

The only man who is really free is the one
who can turn down an invitation to
dinner without giving an excuse.
Jules Renard

Excuses are the nails used to build a
house of failure.
Don Wilder

He who excuses himself accuses himself.
Gabriel Meurier

Never complain. Never explain.
Henry Ford

He that is good for making excuses is seldom good for anything else.
Benjamin Franklin

There aren't nearly enough crutches in the world for all the lame excuses.
Marcus Stroup

For many people, an excuse is better than an achievement because an achievement, no matter how great, leaves you having to prove yourself again in the future; but an excuse can last for life.
Eric Hoffer

A bad workman always blames his tools. Bad excuses are worse than none.
Thomas Fuller

Justifying a fault doubles it.
French Proverb

Don't make excuses—make good.
Elbert Hubbard

Don't look for excuses to lose.
Look for excuses to win.
Chi Chi Rodriguez

Experience

Education is when you read the fine print.
Experience is what you get if you don't.
Pete Seeger

Getting over a painful experience is
much like crossing monkey bars.
You have to let go at some point
in order to move forward.

Learn all you can from the mistakes
of others. You won't have time
to make them all yourself.
Alfred Sheinwold

Experience is a hard teacher because she
gives the test first, the lesson afterwards.

What is experience? A poor little hut
constructed from the ruins of the palace of
gold and marble called our illusions.
Joseph Roux

Failure

If at first you don't succeed,
take the tax loss.
Kirk Kirkpatrick

Failure is a detour, not a dead-end street.
Zig Ziglar

Life's real failure is when you do not
realize how close you were to
success when you gave up.

Defeat is not bitter unless you swallow it.
Joe Clark

I have not failed. I've just found ten thousand ways that won't work.
Thomas A. Edison

I don't believe in failure. It is not failure if you enjoyed the process.
Oprah Winfrey

If at first you don't succeed; you are running about average.
M. H. Alderson

If you want to zoom down the expert slope tomorrow, you have to fall down the bunny slope today.
Cynthia Copeland Lewis

Failure is unimportant. It takes courage
to make a fool of yourself.
Charlie Chaplin

Sometimes victory isn't an option. And
when you're probably going to lose…why
not do it with style, and maybe, just
maybe, do a little good in the process?

The young think that failure is the
Siberian end of the line, banishment
from all the living, and tend to do
what I then did—which was to hide.
James Arthur Baldwin

Think you can, think you can't; either
way, you'll be right.
Henry Ford

If at first you don't succeed, find out
if the loser gets anything.
Bill Lyon

There is much to be said for failure. It is
more interesting than success.
Max Beerbohm

You won't skid if you stay in a rut.
Kin Hubbard

I don't know the key to success, but the key to failure is trying to please everybody.

Bill Cosby

Fear

The first and great commandment is:
Don't let them scare you.

Elmer Davis

Fear is that little darkroom where
negatives are developed.

Michael Pritchard

Whatever you fear most has no power—it is your fear that has the power.
Oprah Winfrey

All of us are born with a set of instinctive fears—of falling, of the dark, of lobsters, of falling on lobsters in the dark, of speaking before a Rotary Club, and of the words "Some Assembly Required."
Dave Barry

Fear is the path to the dark side. Fear leads to anger. Anger leads to hate. Hate leads to suffering.
Yoda

Don't be afraid to go out on a limb.
That's where the fruit is.
H. Jackson Browne

According to most studies, people's
number one fear is public speaking.
Number two is death. Death is number
two. Does that sound right? This means to
the average person, if you go to a funeral,
you're better off in the casket
than doing the eulogy.
Jerry Seinfeld

Fear is a sickness that only the
victim can cure.

It's time to stop being gripped by fear and to start gripping God.

Forgetfulness

A clear conscience is usually the sign of a bad memory.

Why can we remember the tiniest detail that has happened to us, and not remember how many times we have told it to the same person?

Memory is what tells a man that his wife's birthday was yesterday.
Mario Rocco

Hair Loss

Inflation is when you pay fifteen dollars
for the ten-dollar haircut you used to get
for five dollars when you had hair.
Sam Ewing

A hair in the head is worth
two in the brush.
Don Herold

Babies haven't any hair; old men's heads
are just as bare; between the cradle and
the grave lie a haircut and a shave.
Samuel Hoffenstein

Better a bald head than no head at all.
Austin O'Malley

How you lose or keep your hair depends
on how wisely you choose your parents.
Edward R. Nida

Intolerance is the "Do Not Touch" sign on
something that cannot bear touching. We
do not mind having our hair ruffled, but
we will not tolerate any familiarity with
the toupee which covers our baldness.
Eric Hoffer

When others kid me about being bald, I simply tell them that the way I figure it, the good Lord only gave men so many hormones, and if others want to waste theirs on growing hair, that's up to them.
John Glenn

There's one thing about baldness—it's neat.
Don Herold

Drain clogged with what once was your hairline? Friends complaining about the reflection off your scalp? Women observing, "He's awfully cute ... too bad he's losing his hair"? Balderdash. Skin is in, so take pride in your pate.
Richard Sandomir

I don't care if they call me "baldie" or "chrome dome." God took an eraser and brushed my head clean. I'd rather be bald on top than bald inside.
Joe Garagiola

I don't consider myself bald.
I'm just taller than my hair.
Seneca

Experience is a comb which nature gives to men when they are bald.

A man is usually bald four or five years before he knows it.
Ed Howe

I cut my own hair. I got sick of barbers
because they talk too much. And
too much of their talk was about
my hair coming out.
Robert Frost

Hate

Hating people is like burning down your
own house to get rid of a rat.
Henry Emerson Fosdick

The more one is hated, I find,
the happier one is.
Louis Ferdinand Celine

Hatred is one long wait.
René Maran

All men kill the thing they hate, too,
unless, of course, it kills them first.
James Thurber

If malice or envy were tangible and
had a shape, it would be the
shape of a boomerang.
Charley Reese

Hate is a cancer that spreads
one cell at a time.
Dave Pelzer

If, when you charged a person with his faults, you credited him with his virtues too, you would probably like everybody.
Lawrence G. Lovasik

Health

Those obsessed with health are not healthy; the first requisite of good health is a certain calculated carelessness about oneself.
Sydney J. Harris

The only way to keep your health is to eat what you don't want, drink what you don't like, and do what you'd rather not.
Mark Twain

So many people spend their health gaining wealth, and then have to spend their wealth to regain their health.
A. J. Reb Materi

A man's health can be judged by which he takes two at a time—pills or stairs.
Joan Welsh

It's no longer a question of staying healthy. It's a question of finding a sickness you like.
Jackie Mason

Our health always seems much more valuable after we lose it.

A man too busy to take care of his health is like a mechanic too busy to take care of his tools.
Spanish Proverb

Quit worrying about your health. It'll go away.
Robert Orben

Heartbreak

I just broke up with someone and the last thing she said to me was, "You'll never find anyone like me again!" I'm thinking, "I should hope not! If I don't want you, why would I want someone like you?"
Larry Miller

They say absence makes the heart
grow fonder, so I figure that's
why my boyfriend moved.
Christy Murphy

—

Relationships are hard. It's like a full time
job, and we should treat it like one.
If your boyfriend or girlfriend wants to
leave you, they should give you two
weeks' notice. There should be severance
pay, the day before they leave you, they
should have to find you a temp.
Bob Ettinger

—

Sometimes I wish I were a little kid again;
skinned knees are easier to fix
than broken hearts.

Relationships are like glass. Sometimes it's better to leave them broken than try to hurt yourself putting it back together.

My boyfriend dumped me—or rather—I allowed him to set me free.
Darlene Hunt

The heart is the only broken instrument that works.
T. E. Kalem

Jealousy

Jealousy ... is a mental cancer.
B. C. Forbes

Love looks through a telescope;
envy, through a microscope.
Josh Billings

Envy is thin because it bites
but never eats.
Spanish Proverb

Jealous people poison their own
banquet and then eat it.

A competent and self-confident person
is incapable of jealousy in anything.
Jealousy is invariably a symptom
of neurotic insecurity.
Robert A. Heinlein

Lies

Never chase a lie. Let it alone,
and it will run itself to death.
Lyman Beecher

The naked truth is always better
than the best dressed lie.
Ann Landers

Tell your friend a lie. If he keeps it secret,
then tell him the truth.
Spanish Proverb

A lie gets halfway around the world before the truth has a chance to get its pants on.
Sir Winston Churchill

Marriage

Before marriage, a man yearns for a woman. Afterward the "y" is silent.
W. A. Clarke

Don't marry for money.
You can borrow it cheaper.
Scottish Proverb

Let us now set forth one of the
fundamental truths about marriage:
the wife is in charge.
Bill Cosby

One good husband is worth two good
wives, because traditionally, things are
valued by their scarcity.

After about twenty years of marriage, I'm
finally starting to scratch the surface of
what women want. And I think the
answer lies somewhere between
conversation and chocolate.
Mel Gibson

An archaeologist is the best husband a woman can have; the older she gets, the more interested he is in her.
Agatha Christie

—

A successful man is one who can earn more money than his wife can possibly spend. A successful woman is one who can find that man.

—

There's a way of transferring funds that is even faster than electronic banking. It's called marriage.
Donald H. McGannon

No man was ever shot by his wife
while doing the dishes.

—

If it weren't for marriage, men and women
would have to fight with total strangers.
Marriage is a matter of give and take, but
so far I haven't been able to find anybody
who'll take what I have to give.
Cass Daley

—

Try praising your wife, even if
it does frighten her at first.
Billy Sunday

A good marriage would be between a
blind wife and a deaf husband.
Montaigne

Before marriage, a man will go home and
lie awake all night thinking about
something you said; after marriage, he'll
go to sleep before you finish saying it.
Helen Rowland

Marrying a man is like buying something
you've been admiring for a long time in a
shop window. You may love it when you
get it home, but it doesn't always go with
everything else in the house.
Jean Kerr

I think men who have a pierced ear are better prepared for marriage. They've experienced pain and bought jewelry.
Rita Rudner

—

I haven't spoken to my wife in years. I didn't want to interrupt her.
Rodney Dangerfield

—

I would like to go full speed ahead, but I'm married to a speed bump.

—

Marriage is when a man and woman become as one; the trouble starts when they try to decide which one.

I have often wanted to drown my troubles,
but I can't get my wife to go swimming.
Jimmy Carter

I married beneath me. All women do.
Lady Nancy Astor

Mistakes

Mistakes are part of the dues one
pays for a full life.
Sophia Loren

I never make stupid mistakes.
Only very, very clever ones.
John Peel

The individual who is mistake-free is also probably sitting around doing nothing. And that is a very big mistake.
John Wooden

Never say, "oops." Always say, "Ah, interesting."

We are all fallen creatures and all very hard to live with.
C. S. Lewis

Laughing at our mistakes can lengthen our own life. Laughing at someone else's can shorten it.
Cullen Hightower

If you don't make mistakes, you're
not working on hard enough
problems. And that's a big mistake.
F. Wikzek

That's not serious; it's just human.
Jerry Kopke

The man who makes no mistakes does
not usually make anything.
Edward Phelps

Just because you make mistakes
doesn't mean you are one.

In the game of life it's a good idea to have
a few early losses, which relieves you
of the pressure of trying to maintain
an undefeated season.
Bill Vaughan

It was when I found out I could make
mistakes that I knew I was
on to something.
Ornette Coleman

Making mistakes simply means
you are learning faster.
Weston H. Agor

Things could be worse. Suppose your errors were counted and published every day, like those of a baseball player.

Admit your errors before someone else exaggerates them.
Andrew V. Mason

You will do foolish things, but do them with enthusiasm.
Colette

While one person hesitates because he feels inferior, the other is busy making mistakes and becoming superior.
Henry C. Link

An expert is a man who has made all
the mistakes which can be made
in a very narrow field.
Niels Bohr

Personal Finance

After looking at the bill for my operation,
I understand why the doctors wear
masks in the operating room.

Our income is like our shoes; if too small,
they gall and pinch us, but if too large,
they cause us to stumble and trip.
Charles Caleb Colton

Borrow money from pessimists—
they don't expect it back.

Happiness is a positive cash flow.
Fred Adler

If you lend someone $20, and never see
that person again, it was probably worth it.
Another way to solve the traffic problems of
this country is to pass a law that only paid-
for cars be allowed to use the highways.
Will Rogers

Budget: a mathematical confirmation
of your suspicions.
A. A. Latimer

If more of us valued food and cheer and song above hoarded gold, it would be a merrier world.
J.R.R. Tolkien

A bank is a place that will lend you money if you can prove that you don't need it.
Bob Hope

What's the quickest way to become a millionaire? Borrow fivers off everyone you meet.
Richard Branson

Why is there so much month left
at the end of the money?
John Barrymore

About the time we can make ends meet,
somebody moves the ends.
Herbert Hoover

I have enough money to last me the rest
of my life, unless I buy something.
Jackie Mason

Today's payslip has more deductions than
a Sherlock Holmes novel.
Raymond Cvikota

A bank is a place where they lend you an umbrella in fair weather and ask for it back when it begins to rain.
Robert Frost

Money was invented so we could know exactly how much we owe.
Cullen Hightower

The time to save is now. When a dog gets a bone, he doesn't go out and make a down payment on a bigger bone. He buries the one he's got.
Will Rogers

Having more money does not insure happiness. People with 10 million dollars are no happier than people with 9 million dollars.
Hobart Brown

—

The quickest way to double your money is to fold it in half and put it back in your pocket.

—

The trick is to stop thinking of it as "your" money.
IRS auditor

Procrastination

Don't fool yourself that important things
can be put off till tomorrow; they can be
put off forever, or not at all.
Mignon McLaughlin

———

Procrastinate now; don't put it off!

———

I am definitely going to take a course on
time management ... just as soon as I can
work it into my schedule.
Louis E. Boone

———

The sooner I fall behind, the more
time I have to catch up.

Procrastination is the bad habit of putting off until the day after tomorrow what should have been done the day before yesterday.
Napoleon Hill

———

The two rules of procrastination: 1) Do it today. 2) Tomorrow will be today tomorrow.

———

All things come to those who wait, but when they come they're out of date.

———

Tomorrow is often the busiest day of the week.
Spanish Proverb

Procrastination is, hands down, our
favorite form of self-sabotage.
Alyce P. Cornyn-Selby

I love deadlines. I like the whooshing
sound they make as they fly by.
Douglas Adams

Responsibility

Responsibility's like a string we can
only see the middle of. Both
ends are out of sight.
William McFee

We are each responsible for our own
life—no other person is or even can be.
Oprah Winfrey

—

Most of us can read the writing on
the wall; we just assume it's
addressed to someone else.
Ivern Ball

—

The most interesting people I know drink
in life and savor every drop—the sweet
and the sour. The good and the bad. The
planned and the unplanned.
Luci Swindoll

If you don't run your own life,
somebody else will.
John Atkinson

Stress

There are two kinds of people: those who
say to God, "Thy will be done," and those
to whom God says, "All right, then, have
it your way."
C. S. Lewis

Stress: The confusion created when one's
mind overrides the body's basic desire to
choke the living daylights out of some
jerk who desperately deserves it.

Half our life is spent trying to find
something to do with the time we have
rushed through life trying to save.
Will Rogers

The time to relax is when you
don't have time for it.

If everything seems under control, you're
just not going fast enough.
Mario Andretti

When you are in it up to your ears,
keep your mouth shut.

When everything is coming your way,
you are in the wrong lane.

—

No pressure, no diamonds.
Mary Case

—

Stress is when you wake up screaming and
you realize you haven't fallen asleep yet.

—

Stressed spelled backwards is desserts.
Barbara Enberg

Stress is your body's way of saying you
haven't worked enough unpaid overtime.
Scott Adams

⎯

When you get to the end of your rope,
tie a knot and hang on.
Franklin D. Roosevelt

⎯

If you aren't in over your head, how do
you know how tall you are?
T. S. Eliot

⎯

It is good to remember that the teapot,
although up to its neck in hot water,
continues to sing.

Taking Risks

I believe that one of life's greatest risks is
never daring to risk.
Oprah Winfrey

Don't do today, what you can't live up to
the consequences tomorrow!

It's a strange world of language in
which skating on thin ice can get
you into hot water.
Franklin P. Jones

It is better to be a coward for a minute
than dead for the rest of your life.
Irish Proverb

Even if you're on the right track you'll get
run over if you just sit there.
Will Rogers

If you aren't living life on the edge, you
are taking up too much space.

The biggest adventure you can ever take is
to live the life of your dreams.
Oprah Winfrey

Teenagers

You know your children have grown up
when they stop asking you where
they came from and refuse to
tell you where they are going.

I have found the best way to give advice
to your children is to find out what they
want and then advise them to do it.
Harry S. Truman

Always be nice to your children
because they are the ones who
will choose your rest home.
Phyllis Diller

Children in a family are like flowers in a bouquet: there's always one determined to face in an opposite direction from the way the arranger desires.

Marcelene Cox

Humans are the only animals that have children on purpose, with the exception of guppies, who like to eat theirs.

P. J. O'Rourke

Temptation

Strength is the ability to break a chocolate bar into four pieces with your bare hands—and then eat just one of those pieces.

All of us are experts at practicing virtue at
a distance.
Theodore Hesburgh

The truth of the matter is that you always
know the right thing to do. The hard part
is doing it.
Robert H. Schuller

Opportunity may knock once,
but temptation bangs on your
front door forever.

Conscience whispers, but
interest screams aloud.
J. Petit-Senn

The good Lord gave you a body that can stand most anything. It's your mind you have to convince.
Vincent Lombardi

Those who flee temptation generally leave a forwarding address.
Lane Olinghouse

Don't worry about avoiding temptation— as you grow older it starts avoiding you.

You will either offend the world and please God, or please the world and offend God.
John Hagee

There is a charm about the forbidden that
makes it unspeakably desirable.
Mark Twain

⟨⟩

Sin is not a product of our haves and have
nots. It is a product of the heart.
Beth Moore

⟨⟩

Good and evil both increase at compound
interest. That is why the little decisions
you and I make everyday are of such
infinite importance.
C. S. Lewis

⟨⟩

If you don't want the fruits of sin, stay out
of the devil's orchard.

Better shun the bait than
struggle in the snare.
John Dryden

—

Honest bread is very well—it's the
butter that makes the temptation.
Douglas William Jerrold

Trust

I know God will not give me anything
I can't handle. I just wish He
didn't trust me so much.
Mother Teresa

—

In God we trust, all others we virus scan.

Trust everybody, but cut the cards.
Finley Peter Dunne

———

Promises are only as good as the giant
teddy bears they are built upon.
Brian McDonough

———

Distrust any enterprise that
requires new clothes.
Henry David Thoreau

———

There are people I know who won't hurt
me. I call them corpses.
Randy K. Milholland

When the train goes through a tunnel and the world gets dark, do you jump out? Of course not. You sit still and trust the engineer to get you through.
Corrie ten Boom

Unemployment

It's a recession when your neighbor loses his job; it's a depression when you lose your own.
Harry S. Truman

An "acceptable" level of unemployment means that the government economist to whom it is acceptable still has a job.

The trouble with unemployment is that the minute you wake up in the morning you're on the job.
Slappy White

Handled creatively, getting fired allows an executive to actually experience a sense of relief that he never wanted the job he has lost.
Frank P. Louchheim

Unemployment is capitalism's way of getting you to plant a garden.
Orson Scott Card

Getting fired is nature's way of telling
you that you had the wrong job
in the first place.
Hal Lancaster

Work

Opportunity is missed by most people
because it is dressed in overalls and
looks like work.
Thomas A. Edison

Nothing is really work unless you would
rather be doing something else.
James M. Barrie

The number one sign you have nothing to do at work: The 4th Division of Paperclips has overrun the Pushpin Infantry and General White-Out has called for a new skirmish.
Fred Barling

Researchers at Harvard say that taking a power nap for an hour in the afternoon can totally refresh you. They say that by the time you wake up, you'll feel so good, you'll be able to start looking for a new job.
Jay Leno

The world is full of willing people, some willing to work, the rest willing to let them.
Robert Frost

Law of the Alibi: If you tell the boss you were late for work because you had a flat tire, the very next morning you will have a flat tire.

Statistics indicate that, as a result of overwork, modern executives are dropping like flies on the nation's golf courses.
Ira Wallach

A bus station is where buses stop. A train station is where trains stop. On my desk, there is a work station.
Jojn Wätte

Employee of the month is a good example of how somebody can be both a winner and a loser at the same time.

Demetri Martin

My grandfather once told me that there were two kinds of people: those who do the work and those who take the credit. He told me to try to be in the first group; there was much less competition.

Indira Gandhi

The brain is a wonderful organ. It starts working the moment you get up in the morning, and does not stop until you get into the office.

Robert Frost

Anyone who can be replaced by a machine deserves to be.
Dennis Gunston

———

By working faithfully eight hours a day, you may get to be a boss and work twelve hours a day.
Robert Frost

———

I'm a great believer in luck, and I find the harder I work, the more I have of it.
Thomas Jefferson

———

Business conventions are important because they demonstrate how many people a company can operate without.

All I've ever wanted was an honest week's
pay for an honest day's work.
Steve Martin

If hard work were such a wonderful
thing, surely the rich would have
kept it all to themselves.
Lane Kirkland

Accomplishing the impossible means only
the boss will add it to your regular duties.
Doug Larson

The golden rule of work is that the boss's
jokes are ALWAYS funny.
Robert Paul

Hard work spotlights the character
of people: some turn up their sleeves,
some turn up their noses, and some
don't turn up at all.
Sam Ewing

You moon the wrong person at an office
party and suddenly you're not
"professional" anymore.
Jeff Foxworthy

I like work; it fascinates me.
I can sit and look at it for hours.
Jerome K. Jerome

So much of what we call management
consists in making it difficult
for people to work.
Peter F. Drucker

Worry

When life knocks you down, you have
two choices—stay down or get up.
Tom Krause

Nerves and butterflies are fine—they're a
physical sign that you're mentally ready
and eager. You have to get the butterflies
to fly in formation—that's the trick.
Steve Bull

Drag your thoughts away from your troubles ... by the ears, by the heels, or any other way you can manage it.
Mark Twain

Do not anticipate trouble or worry about what may never happen.
Keep in the sunlight.
Benjamin Franklin

The task ahead of us is never as great as the power behind us.

You can't wring your hands and roll up your sleeves at the same time.
Pat Schroeder

If you want to test your memory, try
to recall what you were worrying
about one year ago today.
E. Joseph Cossman

—

People gather bundles of sticks to
build bridges they never cross.

—

The Will of God never takes you to where
the Grace of God will not protect you.

—

We experience moments absolutely
free from worry. These brief
respites are called panic.
Cullen Hightower

You can tell how big a person is by
what it takes to discourage him.

Somehow our devils are never quite what
we expect when we meet them face to face.
Nelson DeMille

A hundredload of worry will not
pay an ounce of debt.
George Herbert

Don't fight with the pillow, but lay
down your head. And kick every
worriment out of bed.
Edmund Vance Cooke